P.O.W.

PAIRED:

A fighter pilot and a soldier held captive in enemy territory. Everett Alvarez survived for almost nine years in North Vietnam's notorious prisons. Shoshana Johnson, ambushed and wounded, was held in Iraq while the invasion closed in.

"My contact with my fellow prisoners was as essential as oxygen. It was especially vital through our darkest days and most perilous moments. It fueled our morale and stiffened our backbone. Without it, we were doomed."

Everett Alvarez

"The guys in captivity with me lent me strength, helped me get through it. They gave me encouraging words, and sometimes were just silly. You have to keep your sense of humor or you go crazy, you go absolutely nuts."

Shoshana Johnson

Photographs © 2012: Alamy Images/Walter Bibikow/Danita Delimont: 30; AP Images: 95
(Sgt. Arledge), 73 (IraqiTV via APTN), 90 (Wally Santana), back cover right, 3 right (Seth Wenig);
Corbis Images: 14, 22, 25, 52 (Bettmann), 58 (Franco Pagetti/VII); DefenseImagery.mil: 84 (TSGT
John L. Houghton, Jr., USAF), 33, 48; El Paso Times Photo: 100; Getty Images: 10, 18
(Jon Brenneis/Time & Life Pictures), 68 (Eric Feferberg/AFP), 38 (Francis Miller/Time & Life
Pictures), 79 (Piestewa Family), 65 (Joe Raedle), 61 (Mike Theiler/AFP), cover (Kamil Vojnar);
National Archives and Records Administration/Pomponio/Records of the Central Intelligence
Agency: 35; NEWSCOM: 63 (Sgt. Joseph R. Chenelly), 54, 76 (Eric Feferberg/AFP); Records of
the U.S. Marine Corps: 44; U.S. Naval Institute Photo Archive: back cover left, 3 left.

Maps by David Lindroth.

Library of Congress Cataloging-in-Publication Data

Cooper, Candy J., 1955-
P.O.W. / Candy J. Cooper.
p. cm. -- (On the record)
Includes bibliographical references and index.
ISBN-13: 978-0-531-22553-0
ISBN-10: 0-531-22553-4
1. Alvarez, Everett, 1937---Juvenile literature. 2. Vietnam War,
1961-1975--Prisoners and prisons, North Vietnamese--Juvenile literature.
3. Johnson, Shoshana, 1973---Juvenile literature. 4. Iraq War,
2003---Prisoners and prisons, Iraqi--Juvenile literature. 5. Prisoners
of war--United States--Juvenile literature. I. Title.
DS559.4.C66 2012
959.704'37--dc22
2011003104

Tod Olson, Series Editor
Marie O'Neill, Creative Director
Curriculum Concepts International, Production

Copyright © 2012 Scholastic Inc.

5 6 7 8 9 10   40   20 19 18 17 16 15 14 13

P.O.W.

Two wars. Two Americans.
Held behind enemy lines.

Candy J. Cooper

Contents

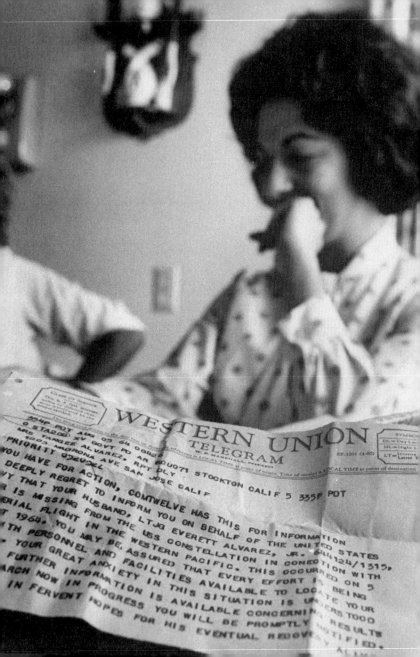

WESTERN UNION TELEGRAM

W. P. MARSHALL, PRESIDENT

SYMBOLS

SF-1201 (4-60)

354P PDT AUG 05 64 09(2)
O STA200 XV GOVT PD AR BQUOTI STOCKTON CALIF 5 335P PDT
MRS TAMBEE ALVAREZ, RPT DLY
1200 MORONA AVE SAN JOSE CALIF
PRIORITY QXXXEL
YOU HAVE FOR ACTION, COMTWELVE HAS THIS FOR INFORMATION
DEEPLY REGRET TO INFORM YOU ON BEHALF OF THE UNITED STATES
NAVY THAT YOUR HUSBAND, LTJG EVERETT ALVAREZ, JR. 644124/1315,
IS MISSING FROM THE USS CONSTELLATION IN CONECTION ON 5
AERIAL FLIGHT IN THE WESTERN PACIFIC. THIS OCCURRED ON 5
T 1964. YOU MAY BE ASSURED THAT EVERY EFFORT IS BEING
H PERSONNEL AND FACILITIES AVAILABLE TO LOCATE YOUR
YOUR GREAT ANXIETY IN THIS SITUATION IS UNDERSTOOD
FURTHER INFORMATION IS AVAILABLE CONCERNING RESULTS
ARCH NOW IN PROGRESS YOU WILL BE PROMPTLY NOTIFIED.
IN FERVENT HOPES FOR HIS EVENTUAL RECOVERY ALL

CAGED

It was the first official mission of the Vietnam War, and for Everett Alvarez it ended in disaster. Captured and thrown into a tiny cell, he was isolated, beaten, and nearly starved to death. What could he do to survive?

Vietnam: North and South

1
Shot Down

A loud blast tore through the side of the needle-nosed attack plane. Alone in the cockpit, Lieutenant Everett Alvarez saw a yellow flash over the wing of his A-4 Skyhawk. "What was *that?*" he wondered, gripping the control stick.

The Skyhawk shook and rattled and began to roll to one side. Smoke filled the cockpit, and emergency lights flashed. Alvarez radioed his flight leader: "409, this is 411. I've been hit! I can't control it! I can't control it!"

An A-4 Skyhawk bombs communist fighters in South Vietnam. Unlike fighter planes, which are built for air-to-air combat, attack planes like the Skyhawk are designed to bomb targets on the ground.

Below the wobbling plane, the coastline of North Vietnam drew closer. The Skyhawk was losing altitude quickly; Alvarez was about to crash in enemy territory.

It was August 5, 1964, and Alvarez was part of the first official mission of the Vietnam War. Three days before, a U.S. destroyer in the Gulf of Tonkin had reported an engagement with North Vietnamese patrol boats. Tensions had been rising in the region for years, and this was the last straw. An attack squadron of 59 U.S. planes, including Alvarez's Skyhawk, was sent to strike back.

At 26, Alvarez didn't seem the warrior type. He was a shy, slight man with dark hair, smooth handsome features, and intelligent, penetrating eyes. Friends called him "Alvie" or "Ev."

As Alvarez began the 350-mile flight from his aircraft carrier, he got a bad case of nerves. It was his first call to battle, and he understood how important it was. "Holy Smokes," he said to himself, "this is war!"

Alvarez had no doubt that he and his fellow fighter pilots were doing the right thing. North Vietnam was a communist state, and communism, in his opinion, was the biggest threat to freedom in the world. It had started in Russia and then spread to Eastern Europe, North Korea, China, and North Vietnam. Entire populations were embracing the ideal of communism—that wealth should be distributed equally. In reality, that was not what they were getting. In most communist states, a single all-powerful party controlled the lives of its citizens.

If the U.S. did not step up and contain communism, Alvarez thought, who would keep it from spreading around the globe?

Alvarez streaked low over Hon Gai Harbor, aimed at a North Vietnamese torpedo boat, and strafed it with fire. As he banked sharply over land, he flew through a sky black with enemy fire.

Then he heard the blast.

As he spiraled through the air, Alvarez knew his jet was going to crash. He radioed in one last time. "I'm on fire and falling apart," he cried. "I've got to get out!"

Alvarez ejected from the Skyhawk. His seat fell away and his parachute popped open, dropping him into the Gulf of Tonkin. He was about to become the first U.S. pilot taken prisoner in North Vietnam.

Lieutenant Everett Alvarez stands in front of A-4
Skyhawks in 1964, the same year he was taken
prisoner by the North Vietnamese.

2
Room 24

From the moment Alvarez plunged into the water, his thoughts turned to his family in Santa Clara, California. He had just gotten married seven months earlier and was deeply in love with his wife, Tangee. Now he slipped off his wedding ring and let it sink to the bottom of the sea. If he was taken prisoner, he did not want his captors to know that he was married; they might use the information to torture him. "Don't worry, sweetheart," he thought, "someday I'll get you another one."

His mother, father, and two younger sisters had been devastated when he went overseas. His mother, Chole, worried that she'd lose her only son, but Alvarez assured her that he'd never see combat. His father, Lalo, worried about the fighting in Vietnam. "No chance, Dad," Alvarez said. "We're not going there."

In fact, the U.S. had been edging toward war in Vietnam for a decade. In 1954, Vietnam was split into two parts, North and South. Ho Chi Minh, the leader of North Vietnam, formed a communist state. He won the support of China and the Soviet Union. The United States backed South Vietnam and vowed to protect it from the North Vietnamese.

For years the two Vietnams had been at war. Communists in the South, supported by the North, tried to overthrow their government. The South Vietnamese executed thousands of suspected communists and launched raids into North Vietnam.

Three U.S. presidents in a row vowed not to send American troops into battle in Vietnam. Instead, they sent military advisers to help the South Vietnamese. By 1963, 16,000 U.S. soldiers and other personnel were stationed in South Vietnam. In the summer of 1964, Alvarez joined them when his aircraft carrier, the USS *Constellation*, began patrolling the Gulf of Tonkin off the coast of North Vietnam.

On August 2, 1964, three days before Alvarez's flight, U.S. destroyers were in the Gulf of Tonkin as well. Their mission was to listen in on radio communications between units of the North Vietnamese

On August 5, 1964, Alvarez took off from the USS *Constellation.* The aircraft carrier held more than 5,000 people and about 85 planes. Alvarez never made it back to the *Constellation.*

Army. Three North Vietnamese torpedo boats began following one of these destroyers, the USS *Maddox*. Shots were exchanged, and the *Maddox* sank one of the North Vietnamese boats.

Two days later, the *Maddox* and another destroyer reported taking enemy fire. Alvarez and two other pilots were sent to the scene. Flying through a blinding thunderstorm, they couldn't find any enemy boats. The report, it appeared, had been a mistake.

That night, however, President Lyndon Johnson announced on national television that the U.S. would retaliate against North Vietnam. American warplanes, he said, were already en route.

Hours later, Alvarez was floating in the Gulf of Tonkin, preparing for the worst.

He was hauled aboard a small boat and delivered to military officials on the shore. His captors dressed him in baggy prison clothing and tried to interrogate him. Alvarez gave them nothing but his name and rank.

For the next week, guards led Alvarez through a series of interrogations and jail cells. On August 11 they loaded him, handcuffed, into a truck.

He was taken to Hoa Lo, a prison just outside the capital of Hanoi. In the years to come, it would become infamous as a place of great hardship, even torture. Americans held there as prisoners of war, or POWs, would sarcastically refer to it as the Hanoi Hilton.

This was Alvarez's new home and he would have to get used to it.

Weeks after Alvarez was shot down, guards made him put on his flight suit and helmet. They restaged his capture so they could photograph it and use it as propaganda.

Guards led Alvarez to Room 24. In his tiny cell, he slept on a metal bed with wooden slats for a mattress. The toilet was just a hole in the ground, and a single light bulb lit the room 24 hours a day. At night, rats would dart out, eat his food, and scurry for cover. A moss-covered bucket, crawling with cockroaches, served as his sink. Aside from the pests, Alvarez was entirely alone.

The prison food disgusted Alvarez. Dinner consisted of a chicken head floating in grease, or a slimy stew smelling of drain water. Sometimes he was served a blackbird lying feet up on a plate, head and feathers attached. Eating brought on severe bouts of vomiting and diarrhea.

Loneliness plagued Alvarez above all else. The rest of the world must have taken him for dead, he decided. He desperately wanted to signal that he was alive, and he begged his jailers to let him write home. They agreed, although every letter he wrote would be censored. In the first of many love letters, Alvarez addressed Tangee as "my most precious wife."

Alvarez invented ways to pass time. A devout Catholic, he scratched a cross into the wall and prayed daily. He put colonies of ants through obstacle courses. He made up math problems, and he created a chessboard and played both sides. He also relived moments from his past, as vividly as if he were watching TV reruns.

For as long as Alvarez could remember, he had wanted to fly airplanes. That dream was born in Salinas, California, where he grew up across from an airstrip. As a boy, he watched planes take off and land. One day a former World War II pilot took him up for a ride, and Alvarez never forgot it.

Still, Alvarez had a long road to travel before becoming a pilot. His family was poor. His grandparents had come from Mexico to work on the railroads and in mines; his parents worked in factories.

Everett learned from his family to value hard work and education. As a young boy, he spent his summers doing farmwork. He took extra classes in high school to prepare for college and became the first in his family to finish high school and go on to college. After earning his engineering degree, he still yearned to fly. He joined the U.S. Navy in 1960.

He never imagined he would end up in a grim prison in North Vietnam.

From his cell, Alvarez wrote a letter to his parents. He was careful to sound positive. "I feel fine and my health seems to be good," he wrote. In fact he was near death. He had lost 30 pounds, and he was so weak that he could only curl up in bed and stare at the walls. "*Toi om*," he pleaded in his few words of Vietnamese: "I'm sick."

Eventually, he began to lose hope. "If they kill me, they kill me," he said to himself. "What can I do?"

The grill in the doors of this cell in the Hanoi Hilton allowed jailers to monitor their prisoners. Alvarez was imprisoned at the Hanoi Hilton in 1964.

3
Friends

One morning a guard arrived at Room 24 with the usual stack of plates. Alvarez lifted the top plate to reveal a huge omelet. The other plates had fried potatoes, fresh bread, and a tomato. Alvarez could barely believe it, and he joyfully tore into the food as tears slid down his cheeks.

From this point on the food improved, and Alvarez regained strength. He would find out later that the guards had planned it this way all along. They had starved him and then brought him back to health with decent food. Now they would threaten to starve him again if he refused to cooperate.

As he gathered strength, Alvarez was allowed to walk in the prison courtyard. One day in September 1965, he realized he had been imprisoned for more than a year. He was so relieved to have survived that long that he broke into song: *"Oh, what a beautiful mooooorning,"* he belted.

Shockingly, a man called out to him. For the first time since he had been shot down, Alvarez heard the voice of a fellow American.

A few days later, Alvarez was washing his food bowl when he discovered a message on the bottom, written with a burned matchstick. He carved his initials into the bowl, and over the next two weeks he checked the bowls closely. One day a

In this photo from 1973, prisoners peer out from behind bars in the Hanoi Hilton as guards stand watch in the prison courtyard.

message read, *Hi, EA, the score is Navy–7, Air Force–7.* It took him a moment to understand: At least 14 Americans were imprisoned in the Hanoi Hilton, seven from the U.S. Navy, seven from the U.S. Air Force.

The news that he wasn't alone revived Alvarez. Not long after, he was transported to another prison, where he was better able to communicate secretly with other Americans. They taught Alvarez a code to tap out messages on the walls. Sometimes the men coughed in code. They scraped brooms, sniffed, and spit in code. Alvarez learned sign language so he could communicate by sight whenever he had a chance.

After months of tapping and signing, real friendships formed. These bonds became as vital to Alvarez as breathing. In their code, the men made a pact: No one would

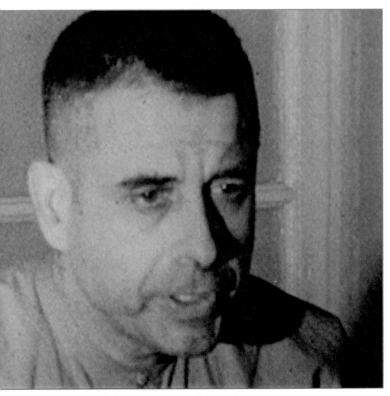

A mile from the Hanoi Hilton, a POW named Jeremiah Denton was interviewed by his captors. As he spoke on camera, he blinked a message in Morse code:

```
 -   --- •-•   -   ••- •-• •
 T    O   R    T    U   R   E
```

go free until all of them were released. They spied on the guards, and if a prisoner was harmed, word spread.

The support came just in time for Alvarez, because conditions at the prison were rapidly getting worse. In the summer of 1966, the U.S. stepped up its bombing raids, and in response, the prison guards cracked down harder on the Americans. They beat Alvarez so brutally that his jaw was permanently dislocated. The men were fed nothing but rice, often covered with roaches, rat droppings, and ants. Many of the men grew terribly ill; they all had the look of starved dogs.

The guards began to torture the prisoners routinely. The prisoners listened in fear for the jingle of keys, a warning that the guards had come for a new victim.

One day the keys rattled for Alvarez. Guards led him to a room and ordered him to admit that he was an "air pirate" who had "bombed and killed peaceful Vietnamese." Alvarez refused.

Two days later, on August 9, 1966, they came for him again. The guards squeezed his arms behind his back and fastened handcuffs a few inches below his elbows. The cuffs felt like they cut through to the bone. The guards beat him and then left him alone to think. Again and again they returned, asking Alvarez whether he was ready to confess.

Finally, Alvarez couldn't take it anymore. "Okay! Take 'em off! Stop it! I'll write!"

He scrawled an insincere apology for his role in the bombing raid. Back in his cell, he grew somber, feeling that he had betrayed his country.

Americans protest the Vietnam War outside the White House in 1967. Inside, President Johnson is having lunch with General Westmoreland, the commander of U.S. military operations in Vietnam.

4
A Cruel Blow

As the years dragged on, the torture sessions continued. Guards would drag Alvarez into a cramped room with blue walls and force him to sit in painful positions for hours at a time. When he moved, they beat him.

Alvarez usually held out for a few days. Then he would give in and read a prepared statement into a tape recorder, claiming that he did not support the American war effort.

Alvarez leaned heavily on his friendships with the other prisoners. The Americans could hear when one of their own was taken away to be tortured. In their secret code, they would drum words of encouragement against the walls of their prison. It wasn't much, but it was enough to keep most of them going.

Even with each other's support, prison life was a nightmare for the POWs. The men got parasitic worms that were up to 15 inches long. They were beaten again and again and forced to make propaganda statements. Two Americans were tortured to death.

In the spring of 1970, Alvarez's fifth year in captivity, conditions finally improved. The torture stopped. There was more to eat, and the men were allowed to play table tennis, volleyball, and basketball in the courtyard.

The prisoners owed their new privileges to developments taking place outside the prison walls. The war was far from over, but North Vietnam's leader, Ho Chi Minh, had died. The new leadership put more effort into peace talks with the United States and wanted to be able to guarantee that all prisoners would return alive and in good health.

As the guards loosened control, they allowed the prisoners more contact with friends and family. Alvarez hadn't received a care package in five years. Now the guards handed out boxes loaded with treasures from home—candy, toothpaste, soap, instant coffee. Alvarez also received a picture of Tangee. He wept, realizing how much he missed her.

The news from home, however, soon grew disturbing. Alvarez's sister Delia wrote that she had begun speaking out against the war. The fighting had dragged on for six years, and many Americans were tired of it. By 1970, nearly 50,000 American soldiers had been killed. U.S. bombing raids had destroyed much of North Vietnam and killed untold numbers of civilians. Critics considered the conflict to be a civil war between the Vietnamese people and said the U.S. had no right to interfere. Protests had broken out in big cities across the United States, and Delia had joined in.

Delia's letter upset Alvarez, but he also believed in every American's right to free speech. To him, that was the meaning of democracy; that's what he had been fighting to protect.

More upsetting was his growing sense that something was wrong with Tangee. He had showered her with love letters, but her last letter had seemed distant, as if Alvarez had become a stranger to her. The feeling gnawed at him.

On Christmas Day, 1971, Alvarez received a letter from his mother that confirmed his deepest worry: Tangee had left him. She had gotten a divorce and remarried.

Alvarez was devastated. For seven years, he had dreamed about seeing Tangee again. Without her, he felt he had nothing, that there was no point in living.

Alvarez fell into a bottomless depression. His prison mates, respecting his loss, left him to his mourning. He paced back and forth beside a prison wall, beating a path in the dirt.

American prisoners of war cheer as the plane carrying them to freedom takes off from an airfield near Hanoi, the capital of North Vietnam.

5

Free at Last

lvarez's depression lifted in April 1972. American bombing raids seemed to come more often now, and occasionally the prisoners saw B52 bombers streak across the sky, bound for Hanoi. The massive warplanes gave Alvarez hope that the U.S. would soon force an end to the war.

For security reasons, the men were returned to the Hanoi Hilton. Hundreds of Americans were arriving there from other prisons. In December, the prisoners decorated their prison cells, hoping it might be their last Christmas in captivity.

The following month, guards lined the men up in the courtyard and told them that the war was ending. They would be going home in 30 days. Alvarez was too exhausted to feel hopeful. "I'll believe it when I see it," he thought.

One night the men were given fresh clothing and the following morning were driven by bus to an airstrip. A giant plane appeared overhead.

"Come on down, baby, easy does it!" shouted one prisoner.

"Man, what a beautiful sight," said another.

The men cheered as the American plane landed. POWs who were unable to walk were escorted on board. Then Alvarez's name was called out. As the first prisoner taken, he would be the first to walk aboard the plane. He stepped forward and saluted the U.S. colonel standing before him.

A sergeant took him gently by the arm. "C'mon, sir," he said, "we're gonna take you home."

Alvarez came home in February 1973, after almost nine years as a prisoner of war. Americans remained sharply divided over Vietnam, but even the anti-war activists treated him like a hero. A crowd of some 100,000 people came to his welcome-home parade in Santa Clara, and the U.S. Navy awarded Alvarez a host of medals.

Over the next few months, Alvarez traveled the country speaking about his

Alvarez, at the far right, arrives at Clark Air Force Base in the Philippines, on his way back to the United States. He and the other POWs are dressed in clean prison uniforms that the North Vietnamese gave them just before they left.

experiences as a POW. He reminded the crowds about the many Americans who had died in Vietnam. "I love you," he said to one group of well-wishers, "but let's never forget the thousands of men who will never return."

On one speaking tour Alvarez met an especially kind woman named Tammy Ilyas. They married in October 1973.

Alvarez left the U.S. Navy in 1980. He went back to college and earned a law degree. He then started working for the Veterans Administration, helping veterans adjust to life at home.

His own adjustment took some time. His back was injured when he ejected from the Skyhawk, and it got worse during the years of torture. He had surgery but lived with constant pain.

Alvarez had no nightmares or flashbacks about Vietnam, but he built an emotional shield around himself as high as the walls of the Hanoi Hilton.

"I was so emotionally drained," he said. "You have so many disappointments and failures, so many close friends you lost."

For protection, he said, he shut himself off from strong feelings.

His two sons, Marc and Bryan, helped him open up again. "The first time I really cried was when my kids were born," he said. "It took a long time."

When Alvarez talks with groups about what he learned as a prisoner of war, they want to know the secret to his survival. For years, he didn't know what to say.

In 1992, a documentary filmmaker flew Alvarez and five other veterans to the Hanoi Hilton to make a film about the prison. Alvarez roamed the gloomy halls and found Room 24. He talked about his time there, with a camera near his face to record every emotion.

Later, during a break, Alvarez sat in the prison courtyard. He noticed that he felt calm, as though he had completely accepted the years he had lost there.

The friendships had saved him, he decided.

"The terrible things they made us do, we shared. If we had guilt, we shared. The anti-war movement, we talked about that. We got everything *out*. And when we left the Hanoi Hilton that day, I walked out of the gates, I looked back, and I realized: *that* was our lifeboat. I left all of my ghosts in *there*."

A woman kisses Everett Alvarez during his homecoming parade. Alvarez had spent eight and a half years as a POW in North Vietnam.

Everett Alvarez

Born:

December 23, 1937

Grew up:

Salinas, California

Day job:

Chief Executive Officer, Alvarez and Associates

Favorite book:

Brave Men, Ernie Pyle

Author of:

Chained Eagle: The Heroic Story of the First American Shot Down over North Vietnam, with Anthony S. Pitch
Code of Conduct, with Samuel Schreiner
Everett Alvarez, Jr.: A Hero for Our Times, with Susan Clinton

He says:

"We have so much more strength than we can even dream of. As long as we have our health and our brains, our mental powers, we don't need anything else."

IN ENEMY HANDS

Shoshana Johnson was an army cook. She never thought she'd see the front lines of a war. But when the U.S. Army invaded Iraq, a deadly ambush put her at the mercy of the enemy.

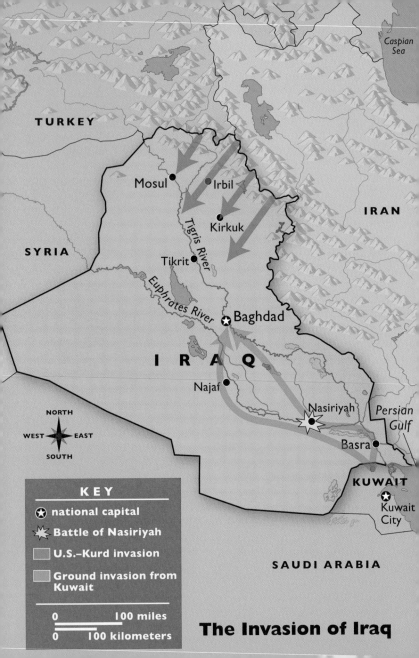

The Invasion of Iraq

Caspian Sea

TURKEY

IRAN

SYRIA

Mosul

Irbil

Kirkuk

Tikrit

Tigris River

Euphrates River

⭐ Baghdad

I R A Q

Najaf

Nasiriyah

Persian Gulf

Basra

KUWAIT

⭐ Kuwait City

SAUDI ARABIA

NORTH
WEST — EAST
SOUTH

KEY

⭐ national capital

💥 Battle of Nasiriyah

U.S.–Kurd invasion

Ground invasion from Kuwait

0 — 100 miles
0 — 100 kilometers

6
Ambushed

Specialist Shoshana Johnson knew that something was dangerously wrong. She stared out the window of her U.S. Army truck as it rumbled through the Iraqi city of Nasiriyah. The streets looked deserted. A stray donkey wandered by the roadside, and a few goats grazed in a patch of grass. But all the people had vanished.

Johnson felt sure they were not supposed to be in Nasiriyah. Her convoy of 18 trucks must have taken a wrong turn. She could feel eyes gazing at them from the rundown

Residents of Nasiriyah enjoy quieter times. In 2003, the city had a population of just over half a million people.

buildings. Were they driving into an ambush? Johnson gripped her M-16 rifle and prayed they would make it out of the city.

It was March 23, 2003, three days after the United States had launched a full-scale invasion of Iraq. The invasion was part of President George W. Bush's response to the attacks of September 11, 2001. That day, terrorists hijacked passenger planes and crashed them into the World Trade Center towers and the Pentagon. Nearly 3,000 people died in the attacks.

Bush claimed that the dictator of Iraq, Saddam Hussein, supported the terrorists who planned the assault. And according to American intelligence reports, Hussein was developing chemical and nuclear arms— "weapons of mass destruction." Bush wanted Hussein overthrown before the Iraqi dictator had a chance to use them against the U.S. or its allies.

Specialist Johnson did not see the point of invading Iraq. The terrorists of September 11 had been trained in Afghanistan, and that's where she thought the U.S. should be using its military resources— not in Iraq.

Johnson also had personal reasons to stay away from the front lines. She was the single mother of a two-year-old girl, Janelle. She had joined the army to be trained as a chef, not to become a combat soldier. At Fort Bliss, Texas, where she had been stationed, she worked as a cook. "Oh, I'm not going," she'd say when anyone wondered about her going off to war. "I've got a baby at home, and I'm not going."

Shoshana Johnson served as a cook in the 507th
Maintenance Company. The company's mission was
to repair and maintain vehicles and equipment for
an artillery battalion in Iraq.

But when the order came, the 30-year-old mother did her duty. She packed her music, a string of rosary beads, her hair relaxer, and a single change of civilian clothing.

In February 2003, Janelle moved in with Johnson's parents in El Paso, Texas.

"Where are you going?" she asked her mom.

"Mommy's going off to work," Johnson told her.

Now Johnson's work had taken her halfway around the world, into hostile territory. Her heart fluttered wildly as her truck wound its way through Nasiriyah. Three days earlier her unit had left the American base in Kuwait, bound for the Iraqi capital of Baghdad. At first they had been part of a single column of 600 large trucks and

A convoy of U.S. Marines drives through central Iraq in March 2003. This combat team had fought off countless ambushes during the first two weeks of the Iraq War.

armored jeeps. Then several trucks got stuck in the sand, and others stopped to help them. The convoy broke apart and Johnson's group of 33 soldiers fell nearly two days behind.

Johnson and her group were from the 507th Maintenance Company. As their name suggested, they were mechanics and cooks, drivers and supply clerks who fixed equipment and supported combat troops. Normally they would travel with highly trained U.S. Marines for protection.

In Nasiriyah they had no one.

The driver of Johnson's truck, Specialist Edgar Hernandez, turned a corner—and drove into a hail of bullets. Within seconds, the windshield shattered. Hernandez ducked his head and kept driving. Johnson ducked, too.

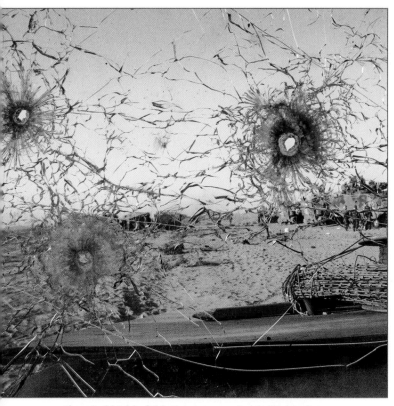

The windshield of this Humvee was shot in Nasiriyah shortly after Johnson's convoy was attacked. Eighteen U.S. Marines died during this battle.

A dump truck ahead blocked the road, and Hernandez tried to steer around it— but he got stuck in the soft shoulder and couldn't move. Then a rocket-propelled grenade hit the Humvee behind them. The Humvee, a military vehicle designed to carry soldiers and cargo, slammed into Johnson's truck at high speed.

Johnson and Hernandez recovered from the jolt. They looked back at the crushed wreckage of the Humvee behind them. Johnson felt certain their friends had not survived the crash. "They're dead," cried Hernandez. "They're all dead."

Johnson, Hernandez, and Sergeant James Riley fell out the door and dove under the truck. As Johnson scrambled for cover, she felt a hard thud against her left ankle, and then a burning sensation in both legs. "I'm hit," she yelled.

Riley dragged her the rest of the way under the truck.

Johnson felt warm blood filling her boots. "Oh, my God," she said to herself, "I'm going to die."

Hernandez fired a few shots from his M-16 rifle, but then the gun jammed. Riley tried to fire his rifle and Johnson's, but neither weapon worked. Now they were trapped, surrounded and defenseless.

Riley and Hernandez crawled out from under the truck and stood up with their hands in the air.

Johnson said a prayer and prepared to surrender.

Fires burn in Nasiriyah during the battle between the U.S.
Marines and the Iraqi army on March 23, 2003. The marines
entered Nasiriyah a few hours after the 507th Maintenance
Company was ambushed. A U.S. general called the battle
"the sharpest engagement of the war so far."

7
The Longest Day

Before Johnson could crawl out from under the truck, someone grabbed her legs and pulled. She screamed in pain. Then the blows started falling.

Johnson lay helpless as a group of Iraqi men in civilian clothes beat her with rifle butts. Finally one of them kicked off her helmet. They stopped and stared at the cornrows braided neatly across her head. One man ripped open the Velcro seal of her armored vest, revealing the outline of her female shape. A woman!

The beating stopped.

The men tried to lift Johnson to her feet. "My legs!" she screamed. "I can't walk."

They dragged Johnson into the back seat of a car. One man grabbed her breast. She screamed again, with all the force she could manage, and he backed off.

The men drove Johnson through crowds of people and finally into a walled court-yard. They pulled her out of the car and threw her to the ground. She looked up to find a man in a blue uniform standing over her. Now in the hands of the Iraqi army, Johnson had become the first black female prisoner of war in U.S. history.

Two uniformed men carried her to a room and set her carefully on a Persian carpet. Her blood seeped into the rug.

She thought of Janelle. Johnson had arranged for her parents to be Janelle's legal guardians in case she did not come home. At the time, it hadn't really seemed necessary, but now it comforted Johnson to know her daughter was in good hands.

An Iraqi doctor walked in. He gently removed her boots and cleaned her gaping wounds, each one as big as her hand. He wrapped her legs.

Three men walked in with a video camera. They pointed it at Johnson and began to interview her.

"What's your name?" an interpreter asked. Another man, who spoke in Arabic, held a microphone to Johnson's lips.

"Shana," Johnson answered softly. She sat in a striped chair, looking bewildered and frozen. Her wide eyes shifted left and right between the men.

"Where are you come from?" the translator asked in broken English.

"Texas."

The interview lasted just a few minutes. Within hours the video would be released to the media and then broadcast around the world.

After the interview, four American soldiers walked into the room—Riley, Hernandez, and two other men from the convoy. Johnson felt a wave of relief; they were covered in sand and blood, but they were alive.

The doctor treated the soldiers' injuries. Then two Iraqis arrived with a stretcher and carried Johnson to an ambulance.

A terrified Johnson is interviewed after she was captured.
The interview was shown on Iraqi TV and then picked up
by television stations around the world.

Fighting off the pain in her legs, she climbed into the van with the other Americans. Four armed Iraqis dressed in civilian clothes also got into the van, and soon they were speeding through the streets of Nasiriyah.

Explosions from a nearby battle shook the van, and the driver pulled into a courtyard. A few hours later, the Americans were moved into a sport utility vehicle, with Johnson lying across the back seat. She decided that they were being taken to Baghdad, and the thought terrified her.

As the SUV passed from village to village, the prisoners felt like circus animals on display. The drivers honked and slowed to a crawl to show off the captives, and excited crowds of civilians cheered.

Like many Americans, Johnson had hoped the Iraqi people would welcome the U.S. Army. Saddam Hussein was deeply unpopular in his country, and many Iraqis wanted to see him overthrown.

But the trip to Baghdad made it clear that the U.S. invasion had enraged a lot of Iraqis. At one stop, a guard opened Johnson's door so people could get a better look. A man leaned in and slapped her. In the next town the guards rolled down the windows and a man spit on Johnson.

They finally arrived at a prison in Baghdad. The captives were given striped clothing, crackers and cheese for dinner, and a thin foam bedroll.

Johnson looked around her prison cell, scanning for rodents or bugs. She lay down on her bedroll and fell asleep.

U.S. Marines advance into Nasiriyah on March 25, two days after Johnson's convoy was ambushed. The battle for the city lasted until April 1. About 260 Iraqi soldiers and 29 Americans were killed.

8
Baghdad

Johnson woke up thinking about her family. Had they heard about the ambush in Nasiriyah? Did they know that she was alive?

The morning sunlight allowed her to see the outline of her small cell. It had brick walls and a single metal door. Mosquitoes had come in through the barred window and feasted on her face and arms during the night.

Johnson longed for her rosary, but she prayed without it—for herself, for her family, and for the soldiers who had died in the ambush. She wondered what had become of her good friends in the wrecked Humvee behind her.

In the morning, a new doctor entered and told her he would take care of her. Johnson's feet were swollen, raw, and still bleeding. The pain was severe. She would need surgery to properly clean the wounds. "I will do my best to care for you," the doctor said. "We must show the world our humanity."

The invasion was several days old. Nearly 100,000 troops—mostly Americans and their British allies—had fanned out across Iraq. Within three days they had captured

Private First Class Lori Piestewa was one of Johnson's closest friends in the 507th. Piestewa was killed during the ambush in Nasiriyah.

the country's major oil fields and were battling for control of several cities. The main invasion force was closing in on Baghdad, and U.S. warplanes were bombing the city day and night.

As Johnson waited for the invasion force to arrive, the small band of prisoners grew. Two Apache helicopter pilots were captured; there were now seven American POWs in all.

The hours turned into days. Each day, an Iraqi soldier, acting as a nurse, gave Johnson antibiotics to prevent infections. A doctor visited her regularly. A guard offered her trips to the bathroom, and Johnson shuffled down the hall. She used strips torn from her army T-shirt as toilet paper.

From her cell, Johnson heard the sounds of warfare: assault rifles blasted away, and bombs screamed and then exploded. The Americans seemed to be closing in.

The approaching invasion force inspired both hope and fear in Johnson. American soldiers might overpower the guards and rescue her at any moment. On the other hand, they might have no idea where she and her fellow POWs were being held. She could easily be killed by a stray American bomb.

Separated from the men, Johnson grew desperately lonely. She wondered when she would be dragged from her cell and tortured. What if she died alone in Baghdad? What if her body was never found? Her parents would never find peace without a body to bury.

Grasping for comfort, Johnson prayed. She thought about the things she had done wrong in her life. She vowed to go home and make the wrongs right. She prayed that she would be able to see her daughter grow up. She wanted to take her to Disney World, be there for her graduations, and go to her wedding.

On her fifth night of captivity, Johnson was blindfolded and hustled into the back of a truck. When they arrived at their destination, guards removed the blindfold. She stood in an operating room, brightly lit and tiled in blue. Two men dressed in surgical gear stood next to an operating table, looking unfriendly.

"Have you ever had surgery before?" asked one doctor.

"No," answered Johnson.

"Are you scared?"

That, Johnson thought, was evident. "Yes," she answered.

"Ah, first surgery in Baghdad," the doctor said, and everyone but Johnson burst into laughter.

As huge explosions rocked the hospital and rattled the windows, the doctors helped Johnson onto the surgical table. They rolled up the legs of her yellow-striped pajamas. She eyed the men warily, but she knew she needed their help. She was feverish and her legs were infected. An anesthesiologist inserted a needle into her hand. Johnson said a prayer and lost consciousness.

U.S. M1A1 Abrams tanks sit under the Hands of Victory statue in Ceremony Square, Baghdad, after Americans occupied the city in April 2003.

9
On the Run

Johnson awoke with her left leg in a cast and her right leg in thick bandages. Two men with machine guns stood nearby. She drifted in and out of sleep until she was awakened and blindfolded once more. She and two other wounded POWs, Hernandez and Joseph Hudson, were rolled to an ambulance for the trip back to prison.

Johnson hardly recognized her prison cell. The thin mattress was gone, replaced by a real hospital bed with a pile of blankets at the foot to keep her leg elevated.

The care and kindness moved her; surely with all the heavy fighting in Baghdad, the Iraqis must have had their own wounded to treat. Yet her captors had probably saved her life with the surgery, and then seen to her comfort. She felt a sudden rush of gratitude that made her cry.

One night during Johnson's second week of captivity, a massive explosion shook the prison. The walls cracked and the roof buckled.

The next day guards rounded up the Americans, blindfolded them, and loaded them into a truck. The driver sped through Baghdad, trying to outrace grenade blasts and automatic weapons fire. The U.S. Army had reached the capital.

The prisoners made it to their new home, a filthy building with a leaky roof. After two terrifying nights with explosions ringing in their ears, they were moved again.

The new prison appeared to be a city jail, and conditions there were not much better. But there were some strangely hopeful signs. On the first day, Johnson met a kind guard who told her that he had 11 children. That night he slept curled up just outside her cell, as if to protect her.

The next day he led Johnson out of her cell to a room where a man stood next to a chair. Johnson stiffened, wondering what was about to happen.

Then the man said simply, "I am a dentist."

He examined her teeth and told her to brush regularly. "When you go back to America," he said, "your teeth will be okay."

Johnson left the room perplexed. Bombs were dropping all around them, and her captors were making sure that their prisoners brushed their teeth?

She tried to take comfort in the dentist's words: "When you go back to America." But in the coming days, the prisoners were blindfolded and moved several more times. Their captors seemed to be unsure what to do with them. With the invasion force in the city, the POWs had become a burden. What if the Iraqis decided to take them into the desert and shoot them, just to get rid of them?

Finally, they took a ride that seemed to transport them out of Baghdad. Their destination was a clean, newly built house. They slept in a large room. Their captors gave them a deck of cards, a chess set, and much better food. One night, they served their prisoners an outstanding meal of rice with dates, nuts, and chicken. There was soda to drink and chocolate for dessert. The food was delicious, but the Americans wondered: Is this our last meal? Will we be executed tomorrow?

U.S. Marines help Johnson to a waiting C-130 transport plane at an airfield south of Baghdad.

10
Rescue!

On the 22nd morning of her captivity, Johnson poured hot tea for the other POWs in the dining room of the house. The atmosphere was quiet and calm—until it was shattered by a tremendous bang.

"Get down! Get down!" a strange voice yelled. Johnson was shocked to hear the order given in English.

The door flew open, and U.S. Marines poured through, scanning the room with their guns raised to their faces. One marine jerked Johnson to the floor and signaled for her to stay there.

Then a marine took her by the arm, pulled her off the floor, and rushed her toward the front door. "When we give you the word, you're going to make a run for that vehicle over there," one of the marines told her, pointing to an armored truck.

"I can't run," Johnson sobbed.

Another marine draped Johnson's arm across his shoulders and dragged her to the truck. She struggled over boxes and equipment as the other American prisoners jumped in behind her. The hatch slammed shut and the vehicle started off.

"Thank God, thank God," Johnson said. She and the other six prisoners began to sob.

Minutes later, they stopped and unloaded. Johnson stepped into the arms of a staff sergeant. She buried her face in his shoulder and cried some more, until a young marine approached.

"United States Marine Corps, ma'am. You're going home."

Johnson imagined that her return to freedom would be as liberating as her rescue. The pain, chaos, fear, and loneliness would lift. She would reunite with her daughter and family. She would resume her work as a cook at Fort Bliss, grateful to be alive.

But life turned out to be much more complicated. During her weeks of captivity, she had unknowingly become a celebrity in the United States, and she was unprepared for the spotlight.

As the soldiers were transported to Kuwait and then to a hospital in Germany, reporters mobbed them at every stop. Johnson said nothing, but photographers snapped her picture. They captured her messy hair and unhappy expression, her face pinched from the pain of her wounds.

When she finally made it home, Johnson struggled with depression. "Why is Mommy crying all the time?" Janelle asked her grandparents.

Johnson felt terrible guilt about coming home when others had lost their lives. Eleven American soldiers had died in the Nasiriyah ambush. Johnson even wondered at times whether she deserved to keep living.

Like many Iraq War veterans, Johnson was suffering from post-traumatic stress

Johnson and other rescued prisoners of war are helped from their plane after it landed in Kuwait City on April 13, 2003.

disorder, or PTSD. The emotional scars inflicted on combat soldiers were once called shell shock or battle fatigue. The condition was given a more clinical name after the Vietnam War. The symptoms of PTSD can include nightmares, flashbacks, panic attacks, extreme sadness, irrational bouts of anger, and sleeplessness.

Johnson had always thought of herself as unshakable, but when her family pointed out that she seemed unstable, she had to agree. She took medication and began to talk with a therapist about her distress.

While she struggled inside, her celebrity grew. She appeared on late-night television. She met Shaquille O'Neal, Laura Bush, Hillary Clinton, and Michelle Obama. She and the other POWs were hailed as heroes at events around the country.

The attention began to wear on Johnson. Some of her fellow soldiers resented the special treatment she was getting. Others whispered that the ambushed soldiers shouldn't have gotten lost in Nasiriyah and shouldn't have surrendered so easily. The comments made Johnson furious.

She had thought she might remain in the army for life. Instead she decided her emotional wounds would heal better if she left.

In December 2003, she resigned from the military and settled with her daughter near her parents in El Paso. She received disability payments for her lingering physical and emotional scars. The money helped her enroll in culinary school, where she studied to become a chef. She wrote a memoir, *I'm Still Standing*, about her experience as a prisoner of war in Iraq.

In August 2010, President Barack Obama declared an end to the Iraq War, more than seven years after it started. The last American combat troops returned home, although some 50,000 U.S. military personnel stayed overseas to support the Iraqi army.

The war in Iraq is still a controversial subject among Americans. Investigators found no weapons of mass destruction in Iraq, and no one has proven a link between Saddam Hussein and the attacks of September 11. Historians say it will take years to know whether the U.S. invasion will help Iraq become more democratic.

When Johnson thinks about the war, her thoughts tend toward the personal. She remembers the 11 men and women from her unit who were killed in Nasiriyah. She thinks about the Iraqi civilians who were caught in the violence.

She also thinks about her Iraqi captors— and strangely enough, what she feels is gratitude. "They definitely saved my life," she said.

She hopes people who hear her story will remember, the next time they see someone of Arab descent, that her captors treated her with decency and respect. Amid the terror of war, Johnson found a little bit of kindness.

POWs Shoshana Johnson and Joseph Hudson return
to the United States. The group of seven POWs
landed at Biggs Army Airfield in Texas.

Shoshana Johnson

Born:

January 18, 1973

Grew up:

Panama City, Panama, and El Paso, Texas

Life's work:

Baker and chef

Day job:

Mother and student

Favorite books:

To Kill a Mockingbird, Harper Lee
The Scarlet Letter, Nathaniel Hawthorne

Author of:

I'm Still Standing: From Captive U.S. Soldier to Free Citizen—My Journey Home, with M. L. Doyle

She says:

"I had some misconceptions in my head when I went to Iraq. Being in captivity opened my eyes. I was shown some kindness that I cannot explain. I was shown respect."

A Conversation with Author
Candy J. Cooper

Q *Could you describe your process for researching this book?*

A First I read the books that Everett Alvarez and Shoshana Johnson wrote about their experiences as prisoners of war. I marked up the books with a pencil and post-it notes. I also combed library databases for newspaper and magazine stories, and for radio and TV interviews. In Alvarez's case there was a documentary that was very good. And I interviewed both people.

Q *Is there a method to your writing?*

A For me the research is a warm-up to the writing. I need to be immersed in the stories before I can start. And then I look for dramatic scenes with lots of action or tension or emotion. I rely on rewriting a lot. The first draft often seems awful, but I try to have faith that I can turn it into something better.

Q *Was it hard to ask Alvarez and Johnson about something as emotional as what they went through?*

A Alvarez has told his story so many times that he can produce his answers almost automatically. The challenge was to take him back to the experience itself, rather than to his previous quotes. That's harder to do on the phone.

With Johnson, some of my questions—about the ambush and the deaths and captivity—upset her. But over the phone it took me a while to realize how she was reacting. If I had been sitting with her, I might have picked up on a pained expression or a nervous gesture and perhaps asked in a different way.

Q *What most struck you about each of the stories?*

A I was impressed by the sophisticated society created by the Vietnam POWs. The tapping code was one example. They also acted out movies they remembered. They taught one another to play golf with the stick used to clean out their waste buckets. They created chessboards and piano keyboards out of scraps of paper. They formed a chorus—and deep friendships. All of that saved them.

In Johnson's story, I was shocked by the many equipment malfunctions. The trucks broke down in the desert. There were almost no working walkie-talkies or navigational systems among the troops. Most of the automatic weapons jammed during the gunfight. Even the map guiding the group plotted the wrong course. I couldn't believe it. People died because of those glitches.

Q *How did Johnson and Alvarez feel about the conflicts they were involved in?*

A Johnson did not understand why the U.S. invaded Iraq. But she understood her duty as a member of the armed forces, and that was deeply ingrained in her family.

Alvarez grew up during the Cold War, when there was a belief that communism was a real threat to democracy. He believed in fighting for democracy. But he also later acknowledged that he had been drawn into a mission that was based on false reports at the Gulf of Tonkin. Still, he bears no resentment.

Q *What was the most significant difference between the two POWs' experiences?*

A The length of time spent in captivity was probably the biggest difference—eight years for Alvarez versus three weeks for Johnson. Alvarez endured torture. Johnson was shot in both legs, but she was treated carefully and humanely in captivity.

Q *How did their experiences differ coming home?*

A Alvarez was celebrated with parades and parties. He was a fighter pilot, which confers relatively high military status. Johnson was also honored, but she faced resentment from peers, which may have been due to her lower rank as an army cook, or to her gender or race. She didn't fit into a storybook version of heroism.

Q *Did they react to their ordeals differently?*

A Alvarez described an inability to get close to people because he learned to protect his feelings while in captivity. It took him years to cry, for example. Johnson still suffers from post-traumatic stress. In my research, I came to see that there's no textbook reaction. Every person responds to war and captivity differently. That's what the stories of Alvarez and Johnson, side by side, revealed to me.

Q *By writing about their experiences, Alvarez and Johnson engaged thousands of readers in the drama of their life stories. How can someone who hasn't had such dramatic experiences have that kind of impact on people?*

A Become a reporter! If you love to write or investigate, if some aspect of the world fascinates you—such as sports or politics or Wall Street or the environment—then you should consider becoming a journalist. It's a great, fulfilling job, and almost never boring.

What to Read Next

Fiction

Fallen Angels, Walter Dean Myers. (336 pages) *After volunteering for the U.S. Army in the late 1960s, a teenager from Harlem tries to make sense of the war in Vietnam.*

Purple Heart, Patricia McCormick. (208 pages) *An American private in Iraq struggles to remember what actually happened in the fight that wounded him.*

The Road Home, Ellen Emerson White. (464 pages) *A young army nurse in Vietnam comes face to face with the horrors of war.*

Search and Destroy, Dean Hughes. (224 pages) *A young American signs up for combat duty in Vietnam to escape his unhappy home life.*

Nonfiction

American War Library—Life as a POW: The Vietnam War, Diana Saenger. (96 pages) *More than 800 Americans were prisoners of war in Vietnam. This book describes their experiences.*

The Brave Women of the Gulf Wars: Operation Desert Storm and Operation Iraqi Freedom (Women at War), Karen Zeinert and Mary Miller. (96 pages) *This book draws attention to the contributions made by women in the U.S. military during the two Iraq wars.*

Ghosts of War: The True Story of a 19-Year-Old GI, Ryan Smithson. (352 pages) *Smithson, who joined the U.S. Army Reserve after 9/11, writes about his experiences as a soldier in Iraq.*

The War in Iraq: From the Front Lines to the Home Front (24/7: Behind the Headlines). (64 pages) *A concise introduction to the causes—and results—of the Iraq War.*

Books

Chained Eagle: The Heroic Story of the First American Shot Down over North Vietnam, Everett Alvarez Jr. and Anthony S. Pitch. (320 pages) *Alvarez describes his ordeal and explains how he survived for eight and a half years as a POW.*

I'm Still Standing: From Captive U.S. Soldier to Free Citizen—My Journey Home, Shoshana Johnson with M. L. Doyle. (276 pages) *This is Johnson's own account of her experiences in Iraq and in the United States after her return.*

Films and Videos

Grace Is Gone (2007) *A father searches for a way to tell his daughters that their mother, a soldier, has died in Iraq.*

Inside the Vietnam War (2008) *This National Geographic DVD shows the Vietnam War unfold from the early 1960s to the fall of South Vietnam in 1975.*

Return with Honor (1999) *This PBS documentary tells the stories of Lt. Everett Alvarez, Senator John McCain, and other fighter pilots held as POWs in North Vietnam.*

Websites

today.msnbc.msn.com/id/35196926/ns/today-today_people
Johnson talks to Matt Lauer on MSNBC in 2010 about her experiences.

www.pbs.org/wgbh/amex/vietnam
This PBS website about the Vietnam War includes—among other things—maps, a complete timeline, details of the equipment each side had, and brief biographies.

Glossary

ambush (AM-bush) *verb* to hide and then attack someone; *noun* a surprise attack from a hidden place

anesthesiologist (AN-iss-thee-zee-ol-uh-jist) *noun* a medical professional who specializes in giving people drugs or gas to prevent pain during surgery

antibiotic (an-ti-bye-OT-ik) *noun* a drug, such as penicillin, that kills harmful bacteria

Apache (uh-PA-chee) *noun* a helicopter gunship that attacks with rockets and machine guns

attack plane (uh-TAK PLANE) *noun* a military plane that is designed for attacking targets on the ground rather than in the air

attack squadron (uh-TAK SKWAHD-ruhn) *noun* a group of attack planes that fly on a mission together

bomber (BOM-ur) *noun* a large military airplane that drops heavy bombs on targets

censor (SEN-sur) *verb* to remove parts of a book, play, film, etc. thought to be harmful or offensive

communism (KOM-yuh-niz-uhm) *noun* a way of organizing a country so that all property belongs to the government or community, and resources are shared by all

convoy (KON-voi) *noun* a group of military vehicles traveling together for safety or convenience

destroyer (di-STROI-ur) *noun* a small, very fast warship that uses guns and torpedoes to protect other ships

flashback (FLASH-bak) *noun* a vivid re-experience of a stressful or painful event

ideal (eye-DEE-uhl) *noun* a standard of excellence or perfection

interrogate (in-TER-uh-gate) *verb* to question someone in detail

post-traumatic stress disorder (POHST traw-MAT-ik STRESS diss-OR-dur) *noun* a mental condition that can develop after one experiences a terrifying event. People with PTSD can suffer from anxiety, depression, flashbacks, and substance abuse.

POW (PEE OH DUH-buhl-yoo) *noun* a member of the military captured and held by the enemy. *POW* stands for "prisoner of war."

rosary (ROH-zuh-ree) *noun* a strand of beads used when saying prayers, especially by members of the Roman Catholic Church

shoulder (SHOHL-dur) *noun* the sloping side or edge of a road or highway

specialist (SPESH-uh-list) *noun* an enlisted rank in the U.S. Army between private first class and corporal

strafe (STRAFE) *verb* to attack with machine guns from a low-flying plane

---

Metric Conversions

inches to centimeters: 1 in. is 2.54 cm

miles to kilometers: 1 mi is about 1.6 km

pounds to kilograms: 1 lb is about 0.45 kg

tons to kilograms: 1 T is about 900 kg

Sources

CAGED

Author's interview with Everett Alvarez in 2010. (including quotes on pages 13, 17, 51)

Chained Eagle: The Heroic Story of the First American Shot Down over North Vietnam, Everett Alvarez and Anthony S. Pitch. Dulles, VA: Potomac Books, 2005. (including quotes on pages 19, 20, 27, 32, 37, 47)

"Bio, Alvarez, Everett Jr." The P.O.W. Network, 2008. (including quote on page 49)

"Catching Up with Life: The Return of Everett Alvarez, 25 Years After His Capture," Sue Anne Pressley. *Washington Post*, November 12, 1989. (including quote on page 16)

"Eight Years a POW in North Vietnam, Ex-Navy Flyer Everett Alvarez Explores Old Wounds in a New Book," David Grogan and Jane Sims Podesta. *People*, February 19, 1990.

"Hispanic Former Combat Pilot Talks About POW Experience," Rudi Williams. American Forces Press Service, October 13, 2004. (including quote on page 29)

"Interview with Everett Alvarez." WGBH Media Library and Archives, 1981.

Photograph by the U.S. Navy, August 13, 1962. The Skyhawk Association, A4skyhawk.org.

Return with Honor, DVD, directed by Freida Lee Mock and Terry Sanders. PBS, 1998. (including quotes on pages 13, 37, 46, 50, 53)

Voices of the Vietnam POWs: Witnesses to their Fight, Craig Howes. New York: Oxford University Press, 1993.

IN ENEMY HANDS

Author's interview with Shoshana Johnson in 2010. (including quotes on pages 60, 67, 99)

I'm Still Standing: From Captive U.S. Soldier to Free Citizen—My Journey Home, Shoshana Johnson and M. L. Doyle. New York: Simon & Schuster, 2010. (including quotes on pages 66, 70, 78, 82, 83, 87, 88, 93, 94)

"Battle Intensifies Around Nasiriyah," Jim Garamone. American Forces Press Service, March 23, 2003. (including quote on page 68)

"First Black Female POW Sets the Record Straight," Mike Celizic. TODAYshow.com, February 2, 2010.

"Attack on the 507th Maintenance Company," the United States Army. www.army.mil/features/507thMaintCmpy/AttackOnThe507MaintCmpy.pdf.

Interview with Shoshana Johnson, *Al Jazeera* via *msnbc.com*, March 23, 2003. (including quote on page 72)

Interview with Shoshana Johnson, *The Derrick Ashong Experience*. Oprah Radio Network, February 13, 2010. (including quote on page 101)

"March 23, 2003: Nasiriyah Revisited," Richard S. Lowry. *OP FOR*, March 23, 2008.

"POW's Father Prepared Her for Iraq," Melanie Turner. *Modesto Bee*, October 1, 2004. (including quote on page 67)

"She Heard 'Get Down' and Knew She'd Be Free," Marcus Franklin. *St. Petersburg Times*, Feb. 23, 2005. (including quote on page 91)

Shoshana Johnson's website, ShoshanaJohnson.com/AboutMe.html

"To Hell and Back," Veronica Byrd. *Essence*, March 2004. (including quotes on pages 62, 92)

"The Wages of War: Iraqi Combatant and Noncombatant Fatalities in the 2003 Conflict," Carl Conetta. Project on Defense Alternatives, October 20, 2003.

Index